The
Petronas
Towers

by Catherine M. Petrini

BLACKBIRCH®
PRESS

San Diego • Detroit • New York • San Francisco • Cleveland • New Haven, Conn. • Waterville, Maine • London • Munich

For more information, contact
The Gale Group, Inc.
27500 Drake Rd.
Farmington Hills, MI 48331-3535
Or you can visit our Internet site at http://www.gale.com

LIBRARY OF CONGRESS CATALOGING-IN-PUBLICATION DATA

Petrini, Catherine M.
  The Petronas Towers / by Catherine M. Petrini.
    p. cm. — (Building world landmarks)
Summary: Discusses the social and economic forces resulting in the decision to build the Petronas Towers and the construction itself.
  ISBN 1-56711-346-X (hardback : alk. paper)
  1. Menara Berkembar Petronas (Kuala Lumpur, Malaysia)—Juvenile literature. [1. Petronas Twin Towers (Kuala Lumpur, Malaysia)] I. Title. II. Series.

  TH4311.P485 2004
  720'.483'095951—dc22

                                                                    2003018973

Printed in the United States
10 9 8 7 6 5 4 3 2 1

Table of Contents

Introduction
City on the Rise 5

Chapter 1
A Symbol of Malaysia 7

Chapter 2
An International Team Effort 17

Chapter 3
Story by Story, the Towers Rise 27

Chapter 4
Gateway to the Future 37

Notes 44

Chronology 45

Glossary 46

For More Information 47

Index 48

City on the Rise

KUALA LUMPUR, IN Southeast Asia, is a modern, bustling city like any other, but one dramatic sight sets the capital of Malaysia apart. A pair of tapering, intricately decorated towers soars upward from the city's center, reaching high above the other skyscrapers into the tropical sky. In 1996, when they were completed, the twin Petronas Towers surpassed the Sears Tower in Chicago to become the two tallest buildings in the world.

The towers were themselves eclipsed as the world's tallest buildings by Taiwan's Taipei 101 in October 2003. The significance of the Petronas Towers, however, extends far beyond their height. With their graceful forms, they defy an architectural landscape of boxy, rectangular buildings. Their unique design takes a Western idea, the skyscraper, and infuses it with Asian Islamic traditions. Even the process of planning and building the towers was an international venture. Today, the Petronas Towers provide an architectural symbol of Malaysia's emergence as a major player in the global business market.

Opposite:
The "crown jewel of Malaysia," the Petronas Towers rise high above the skyline of Kuala Lumpur, Malaysia's capital city.

Chapter 1

A Symbol of Malaysia

IN THE FIRST half of the twentieth century, Malaysia was an economic backwater. Few international corporations had offices in Southeast Asia. In addition, the country was controlled by foreign powers instead of having an independent government of its own. Over the course of the century, Malaysia gained its independence and built a new government. Local companies expanded, and foreign companies started to do business there. As a result, Malaysia grew into a vital, progressive, and independent nation. The thriving economy spurred a building boom in the capital city, Kuala Lumpur. By 1980, modern skyscrapers had sprouted up and transformed the skyline.

Still, something was missing. Every one of those new high-rise office buildings was designed in a Western style known as International Modernism. High-rises of the modernist style were shaped as tall, rectangular

Opposite:
The Petronas Towers were Kuala Lumpur's first skyscrapers to showcase uniquely Malaysian design elements.

Before the Petronas Towers were built, Kuala Lumpur's skyscrapers and high-rise apartments were built in the boxy International Modernist style popular in Western cities.

boxes, with flat roofs. They had no decoration on the outside. Popularized by American and northern European architects, International Modernism had dominated commercial architecture worldwide since the end of World War II. All over the world, the style was the same: Modernist buildings in Kuala Lumpur looked pretty much like modernist buildings in Chicago or Amsterdam.

Malaysians were unhappy about that. They wanted Kuala Lumpur to have a special look, all its own, to reflect the culture, climate, and religion of Malaysia, but they did not know how to achieve that look. Kuala Lumpur's business district, the Golden Triangle, was already full of modernist buildings. There was no space left to create something important and lasting that would look Malaysian.

A Partnership of Government and Business

In 1981, government officials decided to move a horse-racing track from the city's center to its outskirts, because of traffic jams. That freed up a hundred-acre site in the heart of the Golden Triangle. It took nine years to find and buy a suitable property for the racetrack's new home and to create and approve a master plan for the new city-center development. Eventually, those tasks were completed. By 1990, Malaysian government and business leaders knew they had the chance to make a lasting contribution to the city skyline.

The new building complex in the city's center would be a partnership between government and business. Petronas, the national petroleum company of Malaysia, was part owner of the site and would build its headquarters there. Other companies would have offices in the development, as well. The master plan never mentioned the tallest buildings in the

The Petronas petroleum company decided to build its headquarters on the one-hundred-square-acre site that a horse-racing track (pictured) once occupied.

world. It only specified that the office buildings had to be tall, because only high-rises could pack enough office space into the hundred-acre site. In addition, the complex would house a shopping center, a park, hotels, a conference center, a mosque, and apartment buildings. Along with Petronas officials, the city and national governments would be involved in the development. In fact, the project was conceived as part of "Wawasan (Vision) 2020," Malaysian prime minister Mahathir Mohamad's plan for progress.

Malaysian leaders wanted to give Kuala Lumpur a city centerpiece that blended public and private

spaces. They wanted the new development to be beautiful. It also had to look uniquely Malaysian. In fact, it had to both pay homage to Malaysia's cultural past and symbolize its strides into a more global future. Drawing on that past would be difficult. Malaysia had no architectural traditions for building skyscrapers; Kuala Lumpur's other tall buildings were designed in Western styles.

To come up with a design for the first phase of the development, an international competition was announced. In June 1991, Petronas officials chose eight architecture firms from around the world. They asked each firm to submit a general design for the shopping center and public spaces along with a more detailed design for two office towers. The firms had only a few weeks to come up with their plans. In August, they would present their designs and answer questions about the choices they had made.

Crafting a New Tradition

One of the firms chosen to submit a design was led by Cesar Pelli, a prominent American architect. Pelli was intrigued by the challenge of designing two skyscrapers that would be free of the influences of American and northwest European architecture. Since Malaysia had no tradition of tall buildings, he decided to create a new tradition. He based that tradition on ideas from the tropical climate, the local culture, and the Islamic religion that infuses the culture.

Twin towers built in the modernist style were usually designed to be two different heights, or they were

A Prime Minister's Vision

In 1981, Mahathir Mohamad took office as prime minister of Malaysia and immediately began to transform the country. He wanted to make Malaysia stronger, richer, more prominent, and more modern. To do that, he had to jolt Malaysians out of their old mind-set. In the past, Malaysia was ruled by other countries. It now had its own government, but many Malaysians still thought of their nation as weak. Mahathir urged them think of themselves as a country to be reckoned with. At the same time, he found ways to force the rest of the world to take notice.

Mahathir commissioned new civil engineering projects, including roads, bridges, and skyscrapers. To push Malaysia into the international spotlight, he made sure that many of those projects were among the biggest and best in the world. The Petronas Towers, the world's tallest buildings, are only one example. Under Mahathir's leadership, Malaysia built the world's highest flagpole, Asia's longest bridge, and one of the world's most sophisticated airports. Malaysians have also begun work on the world's longest building, a ten-story, snakelike structure dubbed the Linear City.

Prime Minister Mahathir Mohamad transformed Malaysia from a rural economy into a major global economic force.

All of these projects are part of Mahathir's "Wawasan (Vision) 2020," a broad-based development and public relations program. Mahathir's vision sets goals for the nation to achieve by 2020. Most are economic targets, but others address ways to create a common Malaysian identity out of a racially diverse people.

A financial crisis that hit Asia in 1997 posed some serious setbacks to Mahathir's plans for Malaysia's economic growth. Still, he is credited with transforming a rural economy—based on rubber, palm oil, and tin—into a manufacturing powerhouse.

two same-size buildings, placed at angles to each other. Either way, the overall composition was asymmetrical. That meant it looked different on one side than the other. Pelli remembered a principle of Asian thought he had heard in an architecture lecture years earlier. The idea was from ancient Chinese philosopher Lao-tzu, who said the shape of an object was

American architect Cesar Pelli designed symmetrical towers of the same height that would provide a visual gateway to the city.

defined not by the object but by the space around it. This concept, known as "negative space," became a guiding force in Pelli's design.

His clients wanted the towers to be a symbolic gateway to the city center. In Pelli's design, the towers are a visual gateway as well. He designed them to be seen as a single form, not as two separate buildings. He also made them the same height—1,246 feet—in his original plan. That made them symmetrical, like

two sides of a gate. At that height, the towers would have been slightly shorter than the Empire State Building in New York City, and much shorter than Chicago's Sears Tower, which, at 1,450 feet, was then the tallest building in the world.

Pelli's plan for the Petronas Towers, with their identical height and symmetry, made the negative space between them act as part of the design. "This space," he says, "is the key element in the composition."[1] He emphasized that space by adding a pedestrian "skybridge" between the towers, more than forty stories above the ground. The bridge provides a practical way to get from one tower to the other. It also makes the towers look more like a gateway—a gateway to the city, but also a gateway to the sky. "In many cultures, detached portals, or gates, represent thresholds to a higher world," Pelli writes. "This quality is evident in the sky portal at Kuala Lumpur."[2]

Islamic designs are often based on complex geometric figures, whose intricacy is seen as a metaphor for the incomprehensibility of God, so Pelli based his building design on a twelve-pointed star. In other words, the floor plan of one of the stories, seen from above, would look like a star with twelve points. The star shape would echo a form he thought would be noticed and appreciated by Malaysians. The shape would also provide a graceful design and an efficient floor plan.

In late August 1991, the firm of Cesar Pelli & Associates was chosen to design the Petronas Towers. Now, Pelli's real work could begin.

An International Team Effort

THE PRELIMINARY DESIGN was only a first step. Next, Petronas and government officials suggested ways to improve it. Over the next few months, Pelli worked with them to come up with a plan everyone liked. He did not work alone. The team included sixteen firms from around the world, with expertise in structural engineering, mechanical engineering, landscape design, and other specialties. Throughout the process, the foreign firms worked closely with the Malaysian professionals to share their experience in high-rise design and construction. On every level, the Petronas Towers project was a study in international cooperation.

One of the first design suggestions came from Malaysia's prime minister, Mahathir. He recommended changing the layout from a twelve-pointed star to an eight-pointed star. The eight-pointed star, formed by placing one square on top of another and rotating it,

Opposite:
Pelli's challenge was to create a structure that would incorporate Malaysia's cultural past with its future as a global power.

Cesar Pelli's concept of an eight-pointed star, with each point connected by a semicircle, created an interesting external design that also maximized interior space.

is the most common geometric basis for Islamic designs. It appears in visual arts throughout the country —in screens, architectural details, and other decorative arts.

When Pelli learned of its importance, he tried to redesign his towers based on an eight-pointed star, but the shape of the rooms it created was impractical. The star's points created interior space that was difficult to use. Pelli went back to the drawing board and came up with a design that began with an eight-pointed star but added eight semicircles in between the points. This gave the building's layout sixteen "lobes." The shape

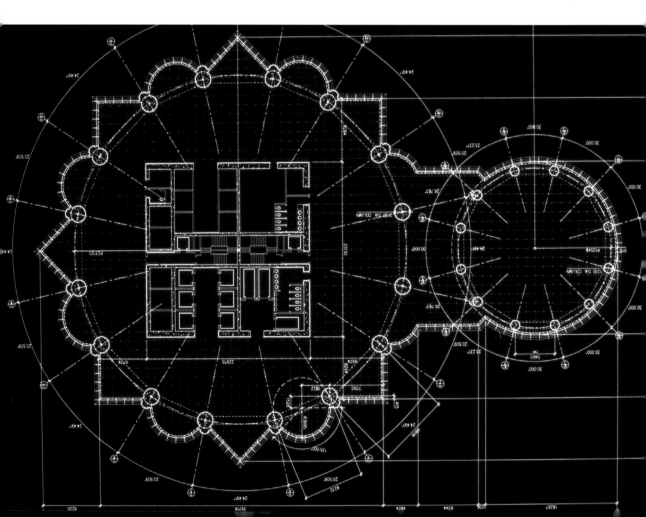

created a more interesting design from the outside and a more useable space inside.

Reaching for the Sky

Throughout the months-long process of refining the project, various design changes made the planned towers taller than they were in the original design. Gradually, the Petronas Towers grew closer to the height of Chicago's Sears Tower. "It was never the intention to build the tallest building, because we always thought a year later somebody is going to build taller,"[3] recounts Hashimah Hashim, an engineer who worked on the Petronas project.

Eventually, the designers realized that the towers were less than seventeen feet short of the Sears Tower. When Mahathir learned how close they were, he asked what it would take to make the Petronas Towers taller. In response, the team decided to build a little higher, to 1,483 feet, to claim the title of tallest in the world.

Building with Concrete

Most modern high-rises are framed in steel, but engineers decided on concrete as a better choice for Petronas. One reason was financial: It would cost too much to import a lot of steel to Malaysia. Structural considerations were also important. Because of their extreme height and slender forms, the towers had to be very stiff. All tall buildings sway in the wind, but too much swaying could weaken or even tear apart the skybridge between the towers. Extrastrong concrete would minimize the amount of swaying. Furthermore, concrete could be easily molded into the complex shapes necessary for the towers' design.

Finally, concrete was a good choice because local construction workers had more experience building with concrete than with steel. Construction was being bid out to foreign contractors, but much of the on-site labor force would be hired locally. It made sense to choose materials the workers felt comfortable with. Altogether, more than two hundred thousand tons of concrete would go into the towers. In order to make enough of it and to be sure its quality was consistent, concrete plants were installed at the site for use during construction.

Though concrete was the primary construction material, it would be reinforced with steel. In all, the towers would use thirty-six thousand tons of steel—more weight than three thousand elephants.

A Tube Within a Tube

The choice of concrete as a building material led to other structural decisions. Concrete high-rises tend to be boxy in shape, but Pelli's design called for slender, graceful towers. Charles Thornton, the chief structural engineer, had to devise a new system for building them. His goal was to build an internal structure that would be strong enough to support the towers' enormous height without making them too thick. He designed an ingenious building plan that essentially made each tower a tube within a tube.

The inner tube is the core of the building. Every high-rise has a core, which is like its spine—a tall, strong,

hollow tube that rises up through its center. Inside it are conduits for electricity and plumbing, as well as restrooms, staircases, elevators, and other necessities.

Thornton's plan for the Petronas Towers also called for an outer tube to support the structure. This consists of a ring of sixteen thick, circular columns of reinforced concrete. Each column is up to eight feet in diameter. The columns are placed at the inside corners

Each tower has an inner core tube surrounded by an outer tube made of sixteen circular columns of reinforced concrete.

of the sixteen-lobed "star" plan. The columns can be seen from the outside of the buildings, but they are so well integrated into the exterior design that they seem to be extensions of the surfaces around them.

Unlike the building's core, the outer tube does not remain the same size all the way up. As each tower ascends, it goes through six "setbacks," points where the tower becomes narrower. That means that the outer walls of the tower—and the sixteen columns that anchor them—do not rise eighty-eight stories from the ground all in a straight, continuous line. At each setback level, the columns of the outer tube are closer together than on the sections below, so that the tube gets smaller as it goes up. Because of the setbacks, each tower has a tapered appearance, more slender at the top than at the bottom.

Breaking Ground

After months of structural decisions and artistic refinements, the design for the Petronas Towers seemed complete. A consortium of French and local companies was chosen to prepare the site and build the foundation. The project, however, continued to change as work progressed. One issue to be resolved was how to anchor the towers to the ground. From the beginning, Thornton and his team had planned to build huge concrete-filled underground piers, or vertical supports. The piers would carry the weight of the towers down through the soil to the bedrock underneath.

Study of the local geologic conditions turned up a problem: The bedrock in the area was uneven. At one end of the foundation, engineers reached bedrock only fifty feet below the surface. At the other end, they had to go down almost six hundred feet. Under any large structure, such piers compress over time and become shorter because of the building pressing down on them. The highly irregular bedrock beneath the Petronas site meant that one side of the foundation might settle lower than the other side.

Engineers could not take the risk. Instead, they proposed moving the towers to a more stable spot on the building site, two hundred feet southeast of the

A thick mat of reinforced concrete, supported by one hundred friction piles that reach up to four hundred feet into the ground, anchors each tower.

original location. The change meant rerouting access roads and redesigning other parts of the complex, but it also left space to add a large formal garden to the site plan. Finally, with that decision made, excavation began in March 1993.

A Solid Foundation

The geology of the new site called for a different type of foundation. Instead of supporting the towers with piers sunk deep into the ground, the engineers decided that each tower would sit on a thick mat of reinforced concrete. Each mat would be supported below by a hundred "friction piles"—long four-sided columns, thinner than piers.

The piles are all different sizes, but the biggest ones are about four feet by eight feet thick, and reach four hundred feet underground. The length of each pile depends on the level of the bedrock in that spot. Because the bedrock is uneven, the piles are different lengths. As each tower presses down on its foundation, the piles transfer the pressure to the layer of soil that rests between the bottom of the mat and the surface of the bedrock. The soil, in turn, presses back against the piles. That pressure is what keeps the foundation from sinking. In fact, the pressure from the soil is so great that the bottoms of the piles do not have to touch the bedrock; they are held firm by the soil above it.

By early 1994, solid foundations were in place for both buildings. It was time to begin raising the world's tallest towers.

Cesar Pelli

PETRONAS TOWERS architect Cesar Pelli is considered one of the world's foremost designers of skyscrapers, but he has done much more. From his playful use of form and intense color in Los Angeles's glass-faced Pacific Design Center, to his own version of traditional brick university buildings, Pelli's work showcases a variety of styles, settings, and materials.

Pelli was born in 1926 in Tucumán, Argentina. He studied architecture at the university there and then attended graduate school at the University of Illinois. He has been based in the United States ever since, but his designs grace cities all over the world. From 1977 until 1984 he was dean of architecture at Yale University. He has won many awards for his work, including the 1995 Gold Medal of the American Institute of Architects, the nation's most prestigious prize in the field.

Pelli's approach emphasizes the importance of sharing ideas and working with others as a team, as on the multinational Petronas project. Another example is the new terminal at Ronald Reagan National Airport, in Washington, D.C. There, he worked with thirty different artists to use painting, sculpture, mosaic, and other art forms in the design.

He admits to feeling a special responsibility when designing skyscrapers like

Cesar Pelli has designed not only skyscrapers, but also buildings in a variety of styles in cities all over the world.

the Petronas Towers: "If a building is tall enough to affect the skyline of a city or town, its design acquires the responsibility of defining a public, recognizable silhouette that can serve to mark and celebrate a place. . . . When it is placed against the sky . . . architecture needs to acknowledge that it has entered a special realm, dear to all and sacred to many."

Pelli's work has been called monumental, but he does not like to think of the Petronas Towers that way: "These towers are not monuments but living buildings that play a symbolic role. We worked hard to make them alive."

Story by Story, the Towers Rise

THE PETRONAS PROJECT involved building not just the world's tallest skyscraper, but the world's two tallest skyscrapers. Rather than burdening one building company with both enormous jobs at the same time, Petronas hired two companies, one Korean and one Japanese—a firm for each tower. The two contractors worked in friendly competition to see which one could finish its tower first. The contest gave builders extra incentive to complete the work quickly and efficiently.

Construction had already begun when Petronas officials made a last-minute request: They wanted a concert hall added to the complex. It was difficult to graft on a major element to the design at such a late stage, but government and business leaders felt it would be worth the extra effort. A concert hall would expand uses of the towers to include cultural events as

Opposite:
Because building the Petronas Towers was such a large project, two different construction companies—one for each tower —worked simultaneously.

27

well as business activities. Pelli and his team managed to fit in an 860-seat concert hall, the Dewan Filharmonik Petronas, on the third floor in the space between the towers. To provide access to the concert hall, they had to redesign the towers' main entrance and add two formal staircases inside. With the redesign complete, the construction teams could get to work on the towers themselves.

Pouring the Core Walls

First to go up were the walls of each tower's core. These walls made up the "tube within a tube," the square-shaped tube that rises up through the center of each tower. Concrete walls are made by pouring concrete into molds. For most buildings, walls are formed at ground level and then lifted to their locations. The extreme height of the Petronas Towers made that unworkable. Instead, the walls were poured in place. The mold for the core walls was a huge, steel square within a square, the height of a single story. Crews began by placing the mold in position at the first level and filling it with concrete. When the concrete dried, the mold was removed to reveal four new concrete walls. Then the mold was jacked up a level, so the core walls for the next floor could be poured on top of the walls for the first one. One story at a time, the core walls began to rise up through eighty-eight floors.

Once the inner tube of each tower had been started, workers began to build the outer tube around it. This tube consists of sixteen columns of high-strength reinforced concrete. They are connected at each story by beams that encircle them to form a ring around the building. On each floor, the columns were cast first—molded in place, like the core walls. Then concrete was poured into molds to make up the "ring beam" that connects the columns. Again, the work had to be repeated at every story, with the columns placed closer together at each setback level.

A Play of Light and Shadow

As the towers rose, a final decision had to be made about the curtain wall—the exterior skin that would cover the concrete-and-beam structure. Designers

Designers built more than two thousand models, like the one pictured here, of varying sizes while they tried to determine what material to use on the outside of the towers.

were still unsure about what material to use for the outside of the building. From the beginning of the design process, they had experimented with different choices and had made more than two thousand models in different sizes. The biggest model was a three-story-high mock-up of the exterior wall, built right onto one of the towers as the walls grew. The mock-up showed what the building would look like with different outside materials.

Pelli wanted to use stainless steel. He liked the soft gleam of the metal and the way it reflected colors from the sky around it. With a stainless steel and glass exterior, he thought the play of light and shadow across each tower's scalloped surface would echo and emphasize the lighting conditions of the tropical climate. Stainless steel could be expensive, though, so plans were also developed for covering the towers in a less expensive metal, aluminum. Contractors priced the work both ways. When the stainless steel model came out costing only a little more than aluminum, everyone agreed its rich luster was worth the extra expense.

Like the rest of the structure, the curtain wall was added from the ground up as the towers grew. Workers began to attach it in late 1994, when the towers reached nine stories. They started at the bottom. At each level, they fastened sheets of stainless steel and ribbons of glass to the structure; then they moved up to the next level. In all, the curtain walls for the towers required about seventy-seven thousand square yards of stainless steel—enough to cover more than fifteen football fields.

A Bridge Across the Sky

Work on the curtain wall was halted briefly in the summer of 1995 in order to make way for the installation of the towers' most distinctive feature, the skybridge. This enclosed walkway between the buildings is one of the world's highest pedestrian bridges. At five hundred and sixty feet above street level, the skybridge rests at roughly the same height as the tip of the Washington Monument. The bridge itself is two stories tall and connects the towers at their forty-first and forty-second floors.

The bridge is perfectly safe, but it is not completely stationary, because the towers sway slightly in the

The skybridge connects the two towers at the forty-first and forty-second floors, more than five hundred feet above street level.

wind, explains engineer Hashim: "The bridge moves up and down slightly, because when the towers move in, the bridge is pushed up, and when the towers move away from each other, it sort of sinks in the middle."[4]

The skybridge had to be built to accommodate that movement. A South Korean contractor took on the challenge. The contractor built the bridge in Korea out of thin girders. Then its five hundred pieces were shipped to Malaysia and assembled on-site. Once the bridge was ready, its installation provided one of the most dramatic episodes of the construction process.

The skybridge was in three sections. First, the two ends of the bridge were lifted by jacks and set in place, one on the side of each tower. The biggest challenge

Workers toiled for three days to raise the main section of the skybridge, which weighs more than 350 tons, to its proper height.

was raising the main section of the bridge, which weighed more than 350 tons. Jacks lifted the bridge, suspending it from eight high-strength cables. The contractor expected to spend twenty hours lifting the structure to the forty-second floor. Twice during the process, however, lightning struck the equipment, which burned out the controls and delayed progress. In the end, raising the skybridge took three nerve-racking days.

When the skybridge reached the proper height, workers welded it to the end sections that were already in place. They did not tightly attach the end sections to the buildings. David Macauley, an author who has written extensively about construction work, explains why: "Since the towers bend and twist in the wind, the skybridge could not be rigidly fastened to them, or it would be ripped to shreds. The solution was to support the bridge on two pairs of legs, which allow it to glide about a foot in and out of the towers."[5]

The support legs are long steel pipes more than three feet thick. During the bridge installation, workers attached them to each tower at the twenty-ninth floor and swung them upward to meet under the center of the bridge, forming an upside-down "V." The bridge rests on the support legs, which keep it from rising or sagging too much as the towers sway.

Soaring to New Heights

Finally, in March 1996, the Petronas Towers reached their ultimate height of 1,483 feet. They had edged past the Sears Tower to become the tallest structures

Pelli used stainless steel on the outside of the towers because he liked the way it reflected colors from the sky.

on Earth. Construction crews still had work to do before the towers would be completed, but to Malaysians, the milestone was a crucial one. It heralded Malaysia's new position as a powerful international business player, and proved at least symbolically that the country could compete with the Western world.

Soaring into the Sky

As designers refined the plans for the Petronas Towers, a key question was what to put on top of the towers. In the original design, they ended in blunted points, like rockets, but architect Cesar Pelli and his team were unhappy with that shape. They wanted the towers to look more as if they were soaring into the sky. Petronas officials cautioned against making the tops look like church steeples, which would not fit with the Islamic-themed architecture. Nobody wanted them to look like the tops of American skyscrapers, either. "The clients preferred a distinctly Malaysian top," Pelli relates in a December 1997 article in *Scientific American*.

He tried many solutions to the problem before he settled on two graceful pinnacles. Each pinnacle is made up of a spire—a narrow, tapered pole that comes to a point at the top—and two balls. The ring ball, near the base of the pinnacle, is a hollow sphere big enough for people to stand up inside it. The ring ball's surface is not solid; it is made up of fourteen pipes that are curved into rings and fastened together. The fourteen rings symbolize the fourteen states of Malaysia. A much smaller ball, the mast ball, sits on the tip of the spire, like an ornament on top of a flagpole. With its tapered silhouette and rounded elements, each pinnacle echoes the shape of a minaret, the tall, slender tower of a mosque.

The pinnacles are beautiful, but they are more than decorations. Their steel structures house aircraft-warning lights and window-washing equipment. Each pinnacle is more than two hundred forty feet high and weighs nearly two hundred tons, about the same weight as twelve large school buses.

The pinnacles at the top of the towers suggest Islamic architectural elements.

Gateway to the Future

THE COMPETITION BETWEEN the two building contractors ended in a tie, as both towers were finished at about the same time. External construction was completed in June 1996, and internal finishing work by the end of that year. In January 1997, tenants began to move in. The Filharmonik hosted its first concert in August of the following year, and in August 1999, Petronas held a grand-opening celebration.

Thousands of spectators arrived hours early to squeeze into a spot near the complex. They strained their necks to gaze upward at the colorfully lit towers, while beams of light shone high into the night sky. The celebration featured a light and sound show, music and dance, and fireworks. After Mahathir addressed the crowd, a Petronas official read a poem written by Malaysia's poet laureate, A. Samad Said. The poem alludes

Opposite:
The grand opening of the Petronas Towers in August 1999 included a celebration that featured a sound and light show, music, and fireworks.

to the racetrack that once sat on the site: "Where a thousand race horses once spurred, forest winds once rustled, now stands sublime the nation's summit, the twin towers, blossoms of the sky."[6]

A Center for Commerce and Culture

Since their opening, the Petronas Towers have been a vibrant center for commerce and culture. They are

Besides office space, the towers include a concert hall, science museum, and shopping center (pictured).

used by thousands of ordinary people who go about their everyday business there. People work in the towers, shop and dine in the mall that hugs the towers' base, watch movies at the cinema there, and attend concerts at the Filharmonik. The complex even includes a hands-on science museum to teach visitors about petroleum.

The concert hall is a showpiece as unique as the towers themselves. The space was specially designed with adjustable acoustics by two American firms who worked with Pelli's team. A system of panels in the domed ceiling can be moved to alter the way sound resonates within the space, depending on the kind of music being played and the size of the ensemble. The result is a single concert hall that is perfect for performances of traditional, delicate Malaysian music—but also accommodates a full European-style orchestra and choir, and even a pipe organ custom built by a German firm. In the concert hall, as in the overall design of the towers, Asian ideas meet Western ones.

Of course, the primary use of the towers is as office space. The Petronas petroleum company occupies Tower One. Other firms, including multinational corporations, fill the offices of the second tower.

Giving Workers a Lift

Very large buildings present challenges that ordinary office buildings do not. Each of the Petronas Towers contains more than a quarter million square yards of floor space, the equivalent of forty-eight football fields. That space was designed to house nine thousand office workers. To devise systems to move all those people through the buildings was a complicated task. The skybridge provides a way to travel from one tower to the other without having to return to ground level. It can also be used as an escape route in case of an emergency in one tower.

The other key way to move people within the towers is by elevator. In any high-rise building, an efficient elevator system is important. In skyscrapers as tall as the Petronas Towers, it is critical. Within the core of each tower are shafts that hold twenty-nine double-decker elevator cars. To get to any floor above the forty-second, workers ride an express elevator to a sky lobby at either of the two skybridge levels. From there, they switch to another elevator to reach a higher floor. The system is designed so that nobody has to wait more than thirty seconds for an elevator. Because the cars have two levels, each car can stop at two different floors at the same time. This allows the elevators to serve twice as many people and to get them to their destinations quickly. Four executive elevators are even faster. These lifts, which do not require changing at a sky lobby, speed from the basement parking garage to the eighty-eighth floor in only ninety seconds.

Ribbons of Glass

Once people arrive at their destinations inside the towers, they can view the city from any of thirty-two thousand windows. Every one of those windows looks out on Malaysia's intense tropical sunshine. Even so, people inside stay cool, and energy costs stay down,

with the help of a unique system of exterior window shades that were designed to be part of the buildings. The teardrop-shaped louvered shades can be adjusted from inside the offices. On the outside, the stainless steel louvers look decorative and add to the texture of the curtain wall's scalloped form.

To wash all those windows, the towers have a built-in system of openings, like garage doors, to house cleaning equipment. Workers open the doors from inside each building, and a long mechanical arm, or boom, unfolds and extends outside the tower. Suspended from the arm is a carrier with an open top. The window washers ride inside the carrier. From there, they can reach the curtain wall to wash the windows. When one section is finished, the boom

Thirty-two thousand windows offer people inside the Petronas Towers expansive views of Kuala Lumpur.

41

How Tall Is Tallest?

When the height of the Petronas Twin Towers officially topped that of Chicago's Sears Tower, many people in the United States felt cheated. For a hundred years, the title of the tallest building in the world had belonged to structures in New York or Chicago.

Some Chicagoans thought the Sears Tower should have kept its status. After all, the Sears Tower, though thirty-three feet shorter than the Malaysian landmark, is 110 stories high, compared to Petronas's 88 stories. If the buildings were placed side by side, a person standing on the highest occupied floor of the Sears Tower would have to look down more than two hundred feet to see the highest floors at Petronas. Furthermore, the Chicago building is topped with sixty-seven-foot antenna support tubes, which reach higher than the Petronas pinnacles.

The controversy comes down to the question of how to define tall. Standards are set by an international organization, the Council on Tall Buildings and Urban Habitat. The council, which is based in the United States, defines height as the distance from the ground floor at a building's front entrance to the top of the building. Pinnacles like the ones that crown the Petronas Towers are considered architectural elements and are in-

The Sears Tower (pictured) in Chicago was the world's tallest building until 1996, when the Petronas Towers were completed.

cluded in the measurement. Antenna supports such as those in Chicago do not count. So in April 1996, the council designated the Petronas Towers as the tallest.

In 1997, in response to appeals from Chicago residents and civic leaders, the council revised its standards. It recognized Sears Tower by adding new height categories, including height to antennae tip and height to the top occupied floor. The original standard for official building height, however, still rules.

moves the workers to the next area to clean. It takes a month to wash the windows of each tower just once. As soon as workers finish cleaning the entire tower, it is time to start again.

"The Crown Jewel of Malaysia"

Ever since the Petronas Twin Towers first reached up from the city's skyline, they have been an important symbol for the people of Kuala Lumpur and Malaysia. The towers represent a gateway between the past and the future—a jumping-off point for Malaysia's entry into an age of international competition and cooperation. Even the nation's millennium New Year's celebration symbolized that idea: On the night of December 31, 2000, fifteen seconds before midnight, fifteen parachutists from all over the world leapt from the towers into a new millennium.

The gateway formed by the towers was not a traditional Malaysian form, but its unique and unmistakable shape is now intimately associated with Malaysia. It has become a familiar icon to residents of Kuala Lumpur. From all over the city, views of the towers appear over trees and rooftops. The structures' stainless steel sides sometimes reflect a deep blue sky, sometimes flash with sunlight, and sometimes are bathed in the shifting pastels of a sunrise. The shimmering towers have been called "the crown jewel of Malaysia."[7] To Malaysians, they are a focus for national pride and achievement, and proof that their ancient traditions and culture can be carried into the modern business world.

Notes

Chapter 1: A Symbol of Malaysia

1. Cesar Pelli and Michael J. Crosbie, *Petronas Towers: The Architecture of High Construction.* Chichester, Great Britain: Wiley, 2001, p. 9.
2. Pelli and Crosbie, *Petronas Towers,* p. 9.

Chapter 2: An International Team Effort

3. Quoted in David Macauley, *Building Big: Skyscrapers.* South Burlington, VT: WGBH Boston Video, 2000.

Chapter 3: Story by Story, the Towers Rise

4. Quoted in Macauley, *Building Big.*
5. Macauley, *Building Big.*

Chapter 4: Gateway to the Future

6. Petronas Twin Towers, "Grand Opening." www.kiat.net.
7. Macauley, *Building Big.*

Chronology

1981 The Malaysian government decides to relocate a racetrack, the Selangor Turf Club, away from Kuala Lumpur's business district.

1990 The old racetrack site is approved for mixed-use development. A master plan is created.

1991 A design competition is held for two towers, a shopping center, and public space. Cesar Pelli's design is chosen.

1993 Excavation begins for the towers' foundations.

1994 The foundations are completed. Construction contracts for the towers are awarded to two bidders; construction begins.

1995 Skybridge is assembled and lifted into place.

1996 The towers are completed. The Council on Tall Buildings and Urban Habitat declares them the world's tallest buildings.

1997 The first tenants move in.

1998 The Dewan Filharmonik Petronas hosts its first concert.

1999 Mahathir Mohamad presides over grand-opening ceremonies.

Glossary

acoustics—the qualities of an enclosed space that affect the way sounds, especially music, are heard there

architect—a person who designs buildings or other structures and advises builders about how to construct them

bedrock—solid rock beneath the ground

concrete—a building material made from cement, water, and sand or gravel, which can be poured into a form, or mold, to create a solid structure

curtain wall—an outside wall that encloses the structure of a building but does not support any of the weight

finishing work—the decorating and other fine detail work required as the final steps in a construction job

foundation—the underlying part of a building, which supports the rest of the structure

friction—when two objects move against each other, the pressure that causes their movement to slow or stop

geology—the study of Earth's structure, especially its rocks

girder—a long metal beam, often built up from smaller pieces, that is used for strength and support in large buildings and other structures

louver—a fixed or movable horizontal slat for controlling how much light can enter an opening

mosque—an Islamic place of worship

pier—in construction, a large vertical support beam

pile—a narrow column of steel or concrete driven into the ground to form part of a foundation

pinnacle—a vertical, tapering architectural piece that sits at the top of a building for decoration but can also be used for such things as holding aircraft-warning lights

semicircle—half of a circle

stainless steel—steel with certain other metals added to it, which make it resistant to rust and other kinds of weathering.

structural engineer—a person who designs the way a building is put together and oversees its construction

Western—coming from or influenced by Europe, North America, or South America

For More Information

Books

Judith Dupre, *Skyscrapers: A History of the World's Most Famous and Important Skyscrapers.* New York: Black Dog & Leventhal, 1996.

David Macauley, *Building Big.* Boston: Houghton Mifflin, 2000.

Chris Oxlade, *Skyscrapers and Towers.* Austin, TX: Steck-Vaughn, 1997.

Cesar Pelli and Michael J. Crosbie, *Petronas Towers: The Architecture of High Construction.* Chichester, Great Britain: Wiley, 2001.

Philip Sauvain, *How We Build Skyscrapers.* Ada, OK: GEC Garrett, 1990.

Video

David Macauley, *Building Big: Skyscrapers.* South Burlington, VT: WGBH Boston Video, 2000.

Websites

Building Big: All About Skyscrapers (www.pbs.org). The companion website to the PBS series explains skyscraper basics and features several well-known skyscrapers, including the Petronas Twin Towers. Includes a lab section on how buildings resist the wind and other forces.

KLCC Group of Companies, (www.klcc.com.my). This official website of the Kuala Lumpur City Centre has a wealth of information, photos, and diagrams of the Petronas Twin Towers.

Petronas Corporation (www.petronas.com.my). Petronas's official website includes details on the design and construction of the towers. From the home page, click on "Corporate"; then click on "Company Background" and "Twin Towers."

Skyscrapers.com (www.skyscrapers.com). This site provides photos and information on the Petronas Towers and thousands of other skyscrapers around the world, and it includes a list of the two hundred tallest.

Index

acoustics, 39
aluminum, 30
architecture, 25
asymmetry, 13

bedrock, 22–24

civil engineering projects, 12
commerce and culture, 27–28, 38–39
concert hall, 27–28, 39
concrete, 19–20, 28
core walls, 28–29
Council on Tall Buildings and Urban Habitat, 42
curtain wall, 28–29, 30, 41

elevator, 40
Empire State Building, 15

foundation, 22–24

Golden Triangle, 9

height, 5, 12, 15, 19, 33–34, 35, 42

International Modernism, 7–9

Islamic design, 5, 11, 15, 18, 35

Kuala Lumpur, 5, 7, 9, 10–11, 43

Lao-tzu, 13
light and shadow, 29–30

Mahathir bin Mohamad, 10, 12, 17, 37
Malaysia, 5, 7, 12, 43
minaret, 35
modernist style, 7–9, 11

negative space, 14, 15

office space, 9–10, 39

Pelli, Cesar, 11, 13–15, 25, 28, 30, 35, 39
Petronas petroleum company, 9, 10, 39
Petronas Towers
construction, 27–34
design, 11–12, 17–19, 21–22
grand opening, 37–38
height, 5, 15, 19, 33–34, 35, 42
site preparation, 22–24
top, 35
pinnacle, 35, 42

racetrack, 9, 38

Sears Tower, 5, 15, 19, 33–34, 42
site preparation, 22–24
skybridge, 15, 19, 31–33, 40
skyscrapers, 5, 7, 11, 12, 25, 27, 40
stainless steel, 30, 41, 43
star design, 15, 17–18
steel, 19, 20
sway, 19, 31–32

Thornton, Charles, 20–22
tube within a tube, 20–22, 28–29
twin towers, 5, 11, 27

Wawasan (Vision) 2020, 10, 12
wind, 19, 32, 33
windows, 40–41, 43